Young Heroes

# Mattie Stepanek

## Inspirational Poet

Leanne K. Currie-McGhee

**KIDHAVEN PRESS**
*A part of Gale, Cengage Learning*

GALE
CENGAGE Learning

Detroit • New York • San Francisco • New Haven, Conn • Waterville, Maine • London

Acknowledgements

COPYRIGHTED EXCERPTS IN *Young Heroes: Mattie Stepanek: Inspirational Poet*, WERE REPRO-
DUCED FROM THE FOLLOWING BOOKS:

Mattie J.T. Stepanek, Heartsongs, Lorton, VA: VSP Books, 2001. Copyright © 2001 by Matthew
Joseph Thaddeus Stepanek. All rights reserved. Reproduced by permission of Hyperion Books
For Children.—Mattie J.T. Stepanek, Journey Through Heartsongs, Lorton, VA: VSP Books,
2001. Copyright © 2001 by Matthew Joseph Thaddeus Stepanek. All rights reserved. Reproduced by permission of Hyperion Books For Children.—Mattie J.T. Stepanek, Reflections of a
Peacemaker: A Portrait Through Heartsongs, Kansas City, MO: Andrews McMeel Publishing,
2005. Copyright © 2005 by Jennifer Smith Stepanek. All rights reserved. Reproduced with permission of Jennifer Stepanek.—Mattie J.T. Stepanek, Hope Through Heartsongs, New York, NY:
Hyperion, 2002. Copyright © 2002 Mattie J.T. Stepanek. All rights reserved. Reproduced by permission of Hyperion Books For Children.—Mattie J.T. Stepanek, Just Peace: A Message of Hope,
Kansas City, MO: Andrews McMeel Publishing, 2006. Just Peace copyright © 2006 by Jennifer
Smith Stepanek. All rights reserved. Reproduced with permission of Jennifer Stepanek.

*For more information, contact:*
KidHaven Press
27500 Drake Rd.
Farmington Hills, MI 48331-3535
Or you can visit our Internet site at gale.cengage.com

LIBRARY OF CONGRESS CATALOGING-IN-PUBLICATION DATA

Currie-McGhee, Leanne K.
  Mattie Stepanek : inspirational poet / by Leanne K. Currie-McGhee.
    p. cm. — (Young heroes)
  Includes bibliographical references and index.
  ISBN-13: 978-0-7377-3637-3 (hardcover)
  1. Stepanek, Mattie J. T. (Mattie Joseph Thaddeus)—Juvenile literature. 2. Poets,
American—20th century—Biography—Juvenile literature. I. Title.
  PS3619.T4765Z67 2007
  811'.54—dc22
  [B]
                                                                  2007022925

ISBN-10: 0-7377-3637-2

Printed in the United States of America
2 3 4 5 6 7 12 11 10 09 08

# Contents

# Introducing Mattie Stepanek

"**M**y wife and I have been to more than 120 nations. And we have known kings and queens, and we've known presidents and prime ministers, but the most extraordinary person whom I have ever known in my life is Mattie Stepanek."[1] Former U.S. president Jimmy Carter spoke these words on June 28, 2004, at Mattie J.T. Stepanek's funeral. Mattie, just thirteen years old, had died six days earlier from **dysautonomic mitochondrial myopathy**, a form of **neuromuscular** disease.

Mattie earned the respect of Carter and millions of people around the world because of how he lived his life. Despite Mattie's physical and personal hardships, he worked to bring joy, peace, and hope to people. His message was that peace is possible if people choose to make it something that really matters. Mattie used his writing and speaking talents to spread this message.

Through his poetry and public appearances, Mattie Stepanek provided a message of peace, hope, and inspiration to the world.

Mattie published six books of poetry and collaborated with Carter to publish a book of essays about peace. His books became best sellers. As a result, Mattie appeared on television programs such as *The Oprah Winfrey Show*, *Good Morning America*, and *Larry King Live*. Mattie used his fame to express his belief that even the smallest gestures, such as taking the time to say hello to someone, can make the world a better place.

Dr. Maya Angelou, well-known poet and **humanitarian**, described both Mattie's beliefs and his impact on the world:

> He believed that the human spirit could overcome wars, and rumors of wars, hate, destruction, cruelty, brutality. He thought that love cures things. I do, too, so we had no difficulty coming together and holding hands. One thing I know is that spirit never dies. I am grateful to Mattie Stepanek for coming here, for being here, for being present while he was here. And I'm grateful that his spirit remains with us. I am grateful I know this is a better world because of Mattie Stepanek.[2]

# Chapter One

# Coping with Tragedy

Doctors did not have much hope for Matthew Joseph Stepanek when he was born. Matthew, called Mattie, was born on July 17, 1990. The doctors did not believe that Mattie would live long, because he was born with the same severe health problems as his older sister and two brothers.

Mattie's older sister, Katie, was born on December 10, 1985. She could not breathe on her own. Katie spent most of her life hooked to machines that breathed for her and made her heart beat. Katie died when she was only nineteen months old.

Doctors said that there was little chance a second child would have the same health problems that Katie had. They were wrong. A month after Katie died, Stevie was born. To everyone's dismay, he too suffered from the same illness as Katie. Stevie was placed on life support machines. At the age of six months, Stevie died.

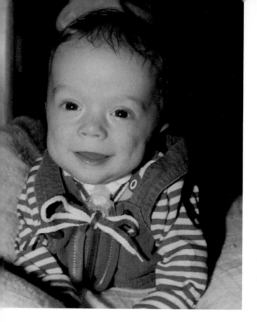

Mattie was born on July 17, 1990. He was born with severe health problems but managed to exceed the expectations of his doctors.

A third child, Jamie, was born in 1989. Like Katie and Stevie, he could not breathe on his own. Jamie required machines and medicines for his body to function.

## Meant to Be

Mattie's mother, Jennifer Stepanek, called Jeni, decided not to have any more children. She was afraid another child would be born with the same disease. Yet she discovered she was pregnant shortly before Jamie's first birthday. Stepanek says she was shocked because she had decided that she was "not going to keep bringing children into the world to suffer and die. But evidently Mattie's a spirit that was meant to be."[3]

When Mattie was born, he immediately experienced the same problems as his siblings. Doctors thought it unlikely that he would live long. However, Mattie survived the night, then weeks, then months, and then years.

## A Diagnosis

After Mattie's birth, doctors diagnosed his and his brother Jamie's medical problem. They both suffered from a disease related to **muscular dystrophy** called dysautonomic mitochondrial myopathy. Doctors also determined that Katie and Stevie had died of the disease.

Dysautonomic mitochondrial myopathy is a disease that interrupts the body's automatic functions, such as breathing, heart rate, **digestion**, and body temperature. This meant that Mattie's brain and body did not remember to breathe, keep his heart beating at the right pace, keep his blood pressure at the right level, or digest certain foods. Children born with this disorder rarely live past their toddler years.

In Mattie's early years, he needed intensive medical care, including a **tracheostomy** tube called a trach. One end of the trach tube was inserted through his neck into his **trachea**. The other end was hooked up to a **ventilator** that breathed for him. Mattie also had a tube in his chest so that doctors could give him blood **transfusions** and fluids.

In 1992, the doctors discovered the reason that all four children had suffered from the same disease. Jeni Stepanek carries the genes for dysautonomic mitochondrial myopathy. She had passed the genes to her children.

Doctors also found that Mattie's mother had the adult form of dysautonomic

Mattie was diagnosed with dysautonomic mitochondrial myopathy shortly after his birth. Mattie's mother, Jeni Stepanek, was also diagnosed with the adult form of dysautonomic mitochondrial myopathy.

mitochondrial myopathy. This form is not as deadly as the version that children get. People with the adult form can live for years. However, the adult form slowly freezes the muscles. Initially, Jeni needed crutches because her legs were weak. Later, more muscles, such as her tongue, neck, and arm muscles, were affected.

## More Tragedy

Despite the problems in Mattie's life, he had fun when he could. He and Jamie played together as toddlers. They dressed up for Halloween together, shared their toys with each together, and joked with each other.

Jamie and Mattie did not have much time together, however. When Mattie was almost three, Jamie, almost four, passed away. Mattie felt anger, sadness, and confusion.

Life did not get easier for Mattie. Jeni Stepanek's leg muscles weakened and she needed a wheelchair. A few years after that, when Mattie was six years old, Mattie's parents divorced. Mattie and his mother, both suffering from the same disorder, became best friends who had to survive together.

## Coping with Loss

Both Mattie and his mother learned to cope with their physical and personal hardships. To do so, they made close friends. Sandy Newcomb, a friend, became like family to them. Across the years, Sandy and her children helped Mattie and his mother in any way they could.

Mattie and his mother also relied on religion for help. They were active members of the Catholic Church.

Mattie and his brother, Jamie, were very close when they were toddlers. Jamie passed away when he was almost four years old.

They believed that God was with them in dealing with their difficulties. Their spiritual beliefs helped them remain positive.

Mattie found another way to deal with his hardships as well. He discovered poetry. After Jamie's death, Mattie's mother began to write down the feelings that Mattie expressed to her. She told Mattie that this was poetry. Mattie explained:

11

When Jamie died, I was angry and sad and scared and confused. A lot of my early [poetry] was about my feelings after Jamie died, and how I

Sandy Newcomb and her family became very close friends with Jeni and Mattie (standing: Jamie Dobbins, Chris Dobbins, and Sandy Newcomb; front: Mattie and Heather Dobbins).

learned to cope with it. Even though I could read when I was three, most of my early stuff was dictated to my mom. Then she gave me a tape recorder so I could make poetry and stories even if she wasn't free to write them down.[4]

Mattie's poems helped him deal with his sadness. "Griefwork," which he composed just before he turned three, is about Mattie's feelings about Jamie's death:

Today I miss Jamie
I am sad.
Last week
I threw a penny
Into the wishing fountain
At the stores.
I wished and I wished
That I held
Jamie's hand tighter,
And Mommy, too,
So maybe,
He wouldn't really die.[5]

Jamie's death and Mattie's physical problems taught Mattie to enjoy every moment he could. He took pleasure in the simplest activities, such as drawing a picture or building a snowman. Mattie wanted to inspire people around the world to do the same.

# Chapter Two

# Childhood Triumphs

After his toddler years, Mattie's health improved. He no longer needed a ventilator to breathe for him. His trach was removed. Without the trach and ventilator, Mattie did not need his wheelchair to transport the equipment. He still needed extra oxygen, which flowed from tanks into tubes that ran into his nose. However, he could pull the tanks behind him while he walked.

With this new physical freedom, Mattie participated in the same activities as other kids. "I had such an opportunity to do things in life for many years that I couldn't do if I was on all the medical equipment that I had as a baby," Mattie explained. "During those years I learned to swim and dive, I body surfed in the ocean, I climbed hills and trees and rocks, and I earned my First Degree Black Belt in [hapkido]."[6] Hapkido is a martial art that stresses discipline, respect, and self-defense.

Mattie also was able to attend school. He regularly attended preschool and then public school. He went to Mattaponi Elementary School in Upper Marlboro, Maryland. Mattie liked being with other kids and made friends easily. He excelled at his studies and skipped several grades.

Mattie also loved summer vacations. He and his mother vacationed with Sandy Newcomb and her family at Nags Head, North Carolina. They rented a beach

One of Mattie's favorite activities was hapkido, and he earned his First Degree Black Belt in the martial art.

house. Mattie liked to walk on the beach and watch the sunrise.

# A Poet

Mattie spent much of his time just being a kid. However, he also thought about what he wanted to be when he grew up. Early on, Mattie knew he wanted to be a poet. He decided not to wait until he was grown up.

Mattie wrote his early poetry as a way to deal with his sadness about Jamie. As he grew older, he wrote about subjects such as nature, religion, friendship, hope, and peace. He wrote one of his earliest poems, "On Growing Up (Part V)," to express the idea that everyone in the world is part of one big family:

> We are growing up.
> We are many colors of skin.
> We are many languages.
> We are many ages and sizes.
> We are many countries . . .
> But we are one earth.
> We each have one heart.
> We each have one life.
> We are growing up, together,
> So we must live as one family.[7]

# Writing Awards

People began to recognize Mattie's talent. While he was still in kindergarten, Mattie entered a collection of his poems titled *Heartsongs* in a Write-a-Book contest. This contest was sponsored at his elementary school.

At an early age, Mattie knew that he wanted to be a poet. He wrote about many different subjects and used his poetry as a way to express his emotions.

Mattie's book was chosen, out of entries from students in kindergarten through sixth grade, to go on to the county competition, where it won first place.

At age six, Mattie was nominated for the My Hero Project because of his inspiring poetry. The My Hero Project is a not-for-profit educational Web project that celebrates people who give back to the world. In 1997, Mattie's poetry was posted on the My Hero Web site.

Mattie continued to win more awards. In 1999, the Children's Hospice International awarded Mattie the Melinda A. Lawrence International Book Award for inspirational written works. The following year, Mattie presented a bound collection of his *Heartsongs* poetry to the Library of Congress.

Mattie won numerous awards for his work. Several awards came from Children's Hospice International. In 1999, he received the Melinda A. Lawrence writing award, and in 2003, he received the Points of Light Award.

# Religious Inspiration

Many of Mattie's *Heartsongs* poems were inspired by his religious beliefs. As a Catholic, Mattie developed many ideas about **spirituality** and religion. "Faith is acceptance, and faith is a gift," he wrote. "Faith is believing in something even if we cannot fully understand it, or prove it."[8]

Mattie was confirmed at his church when he was eight, six years younger than most children. During the confirmation ceremony, Cardinal James Hickey remarked that he had never met any person with more understanding of religion and spirituality than Mattie. Mattie received his confirmation name, Jude Thaddeus, and became Matthew Joseph Thaddeus Stepanek.

# A Peacemaker

Mattie prayed often. He believed that it is good for people to pray no matter what religion they are. Mattie thought that through prayer, people could discover what God wanted them to do.

Mattie told people that God spoke to his heart with a message of hope and peace. He believed that God meant for him to share this message with the world. He also believed that God wanted him to be a peacemaker as well as a poet. "When I grow up, I want to be a peacemaker," Mattie wrote when he was eight. "My biggest role model is Jimmy Carter, who has been a wonderful peanut farmer, politician, and peacemaker. . . . I would like to work as a mediator and share my poetry, essays and philosophy with others so that they may be inspired to work with other people, too."[9]

## Sharing the Message

Mattie believed the best way to inspire people to do something for others was to set an example for them. Mattie did not have a lot of free time. However, instead of spending all his free time playing, he chose to help people. For example, he raised funds and awareness for the Muscular Dystrophy Association (MDA). MDA is a voluntary health agency that works to end neuromuscular diseases that affect more than a million Americans.

Mattie, a gifted public speaker, was asked to be the Maryland State Goodwill Ambassador for Muscular

Mattie received inspiration for his poetry from his religious beliefs. He was confirmed at his church by Cardinal James Hickey when he was eight years old.

Mattie's biggest role model was Jimmy Carter, pictured here with former first lady Rosalynn Carter. One of his dreams was to be a peacemaker like the former president.

To inspire others, Mattie used his gift as a public speaker to share his message of hope and peace.

Dystrophy in 2000. He traveled around the state and talked to audiences. He convinced people to donate time and money to support people with muscular dystrophy and to cure the disease.

Mattie also read his poetry to audiences. He wanted to inspire others with his words. By the age of ten, he had written hundreds of poems and read them to hundreds of people. But Mattie was not satisfied. He wanted his message to reach millions. He was determined to accomplish this goal.

# Chapter Three

# Three Wishes

In 1999, Mattie's health began to interfere with his goals. He found it difficult to spread his message of peace because he tired quickly. He began to use a power wheelchair to save energy. His mother started to homeschool Mattie because going to school was too exhausting for him.

Mattie's condition worsened in 2001. The skin on his fingers, lips, and feet bled because his body could not process oxygen. His blood pressure and other vital signs became unstable.

Mattie agreed to have a trach tube reinserted into his neck. This was a hard choice. With a trach and ventilator, Mattie would be confined to a wheelchair nearly full-time. However, doctors thought it was the best chance to improve his health.

The doctors inserted the trach, but Mattie did not get better. His lungs would not work properly. Doctors said that Mattie had an eroded airway and could die any day. He was hospitalized at the Children's National Medical Center in Washington, D.C., for much of the spring and summer.

# Inner Strength

Mattie was scared. He was in pain, and he was not ready to die because he felt he had more to do. He prayed for strength, talked to his mother and friends, and wrote poetry to cope with his fears. While in the Pediatric Intensive Care Unit (PICU), he composed "Intensive Sense." This poem is about how he still kept up hope even when he was scared. Part of it reads:

> I hear machines alarming,
> But though they ring warnings,
> Lives are not always saved.
> I feel pain, intense at moments.
> But I also feel the hurt of anxiety,
> And neither anguish is good for the spirit.
> Someday,
> I will leave the PICU, again.
> I will see the sun.[10]

Despite his fear and pain, Mattie was determined to enjoy life as much as he could. When he felt well enough, he played with his LEGO toys and X-Men action figures. He made friends with doctors and other patients. Mattie played practical jokes to make himself and other people

Mattie was determined to enjoy his life despite being in the hospital. Playing with LEGO toys was a favorite pastime.

laugh. His most prized joke item was a remote-controlled whoopee cushion.

## Wishes

Mattie remained hopeful but realistic. He knew that he might die. Before he did, he wanted his three wishes to come true. Mattie's wishes were unusual for a child. They did not include a trip to Disneyland or to meet a famous actor. Instead, Mattie's wishes were about how he could help others.

"I wish to have at least one of my collections of Heartsongs poetry published as my gift to the world," Mattie said. "I wish to have Oprah Winfrey share the message of hope and peace in my Heartsongs on her show because people turn to her for inspiration and direction. And, I wish to have fifteen minutes to talk peace with Jimmy Carter so that I can make sure I am doing all that I can and should be to become a peacemaker for others."[11]

## Heartsongs

Mattie wanted his poetry to be published because he believed this was how he could tell people how to find their own Heartsongs. "A Heartsong is an inner message," Mattie explained. "It is a person's inner beauty and reason for being. A Heartsong tells you what you are meant to do, or be, in life. Whatever it is that we feel we need and want the most in life, well, that is what we are called to offer others."[12]

While he was in the hospital, Mattie's wish came true. In June 2001, Cheryl and Peter Barnes, owners of

VSP Publishing, photocopied Mattie's poems and art-work into a paperback book titled *Heartsongs*. Part of the poem "Heartsongs," included in the book, reads:

I have a song, deep in my heart,
And only I can hear it,
If I close my eyes and sit very still
It is so easy to listen to my song.
When my eyes are open and
I am so busy and moving and busy,
If I take time to listen very hard,
I can still hear my Heartsong.[13]

Mattie read the poems from his book at a reception at the hospital. Patients and doctors immediately bought

*Heartsongs* was Mattie's first published work, and he was able to spread his message through his poetry as well as through public speaking events.

200 books. VSP published hundreds more copies. And the company offered him a contract for additional books.

## More Wishes

During his time in the hospital, the staff arranged for Mattie to talk with Jimmy Carter. Carter phoned Mattie at the PICU and they spoke for fifteen minutes. The two discussed conflicts in Africa and Bosnia and what could be done to bring about peace. This led to a friendship. In the following years, Carter and Mattie e-mailed each other, writing about their lives and thoughts on how to make the world a peaceful place.

Soon after that, it appeared that Mattie's other wish, to have his poetry read by Oprah Winfrey, would come true. Winfrey heard of Mattie and his wish and announced that she wanted to read his poetry on her program when the show taped in the fall.

## Miraculous Recovery

Mattie's friends and family, however, worried whether he would live until the fall. Jeni Stepanek prayed to God, "If there is something that Mattie has, some gift that he has to share with the world, please, please let him live long enough and have the opportunities to do whatever he came here for."[14]

Mattie's condition stabilized, and he was released from the hospital. He immediately got to work. Now that he had a published book, he was determined to share his message with the world.

# Chapter Four

# Spreading the Word

On September 11, 2001, terrorists flew hijacked planes into the World Trade Center in New York City and the Pentagon in Washington, D.C., and brought down a passenger plane in Pennsylvania. People around the world were shocked and horrified. At such a dark time, they longed to hear a hopeful message. This led them to Mattie's books, *Heartsongs* and *Journey Through Heartsongs*.

People were drawn to Mattie's poems because they expressed his life philosophy. "I want people to know my life philosophy, to remember to play after every storm,"[15] he explained. Mattie told people that after they have overcome a hard time in their lives, they must take the time to enjoy what they have.

Mattie was deeply affected by the events of September 11. The loss of firefighters, some of whom were his friends from MDA events, and other innocent people, angered Mattie. However, he believed people must get over their anger. Mattie wanted people to do what they could to stop violence. He explained what he thought they could do in "For Our World," written on September 11 in response to the terrorist attacks tragedy:

We need to stop.
Just stop.
Stop for a moment.
Before anybody
Says or does anything
That may hurt anyone else.
We need to be silent.
Just silent.
Silent for a moment.
Before we forever lose
The blessing of songs
That grow in our hearts.
We need to notice.
Just notice.
Notice for a moment.
Before the future slips away
Into ashes and dust of humility.
Stop, be silent, and notice.[16]

In the fall of 2001, over 200,000 people bought *Heartsongs* to read Mattie's message. By December of that year, both *Heartsongs* and Mattie's follow-up book, *Journey Through Heartsongs*, were on the *New York Times* best-seller list. A major publisher, Hyperion, teamed with VSP to publish more of these books. In the following years, Hyperion also published *Hope Through*

Mattie wrote "For Our World," in response to the September 11, 2001, terrorist attacks.

*Heartsongs*, *Celebrate Through Heartsongs*, and *Loving Through Heartsongs*. All of the books became *New York Times* best sellers.

# Changes for Mattie

The success of Mattie's books brought many changes to his life. It gave him and his mother stability. Before the books were published, Mattie and his mother often did not have enough money. Jeni Stepanek, a research associate and doctoral candidate at the University of Maryland, could not work full-time. She had to care for

Mattie and was in a wheelchair due to her own neuro-muscular disease. Additionally, the medical needs for her and Mattie were expensive.

Because they had little money, Mattie and his mother often lived in dark basement apartments in Maryland. With the success of the books, Mattie and his mother were able to move into a condo with eleven windows. Sandy Newcomb, their close friend, moved next door and helped them with daily tasks.

Another major change for Mattie was that he became famous. As his books became popular, Mattie was invited to appear on talk shows throughout the United States. Despite his medical issues, Mattie was

Mattie's success brought many changes to his life. As a result of his success, he was able to spread his message to the world.

determined to speak on these shows. He wanted to use his fame to teach people what they could do to promote peace in the world.

## Talking to the World

Mattie spread his message of peace as he read and talked about his poetry on shows like *Larry King Live* and *Good Morning America*. And his third wish came true. Oprah Winfrey provided a private jet to fly Mattie and his mother to her show. On the show, Mattie read his poems.

In December 2001, Mattie got a great surprise when he appeared on the *Good Morning America* show. President Jimmy Carter walked onto the stage while Mattie was being interviewed. Mattie was overjoyed to meet his hero, whom he considered a true peacemaker.

## Supporting MDA

Mattie also used his newfound fame to help MDA. In 2001, he appeared on the national MDA telethon via satellite. MDA national chairman Jerry Lewis spoke with Mattie. Mattie read his poetry and talked about his life. After Mattie spoke, many viewers called in to pledge money for MDA.

The MDA was impressed with Mattie's MDA work in Maryland, his speaking ability, and optimistic outlook. The association asked him to be the 2002 MDA National Goodwill Ambassador. Mattie accepted and made appearances nationwide to raise funds and awareness for MDA. At these appearances, Mattie also took the opportunity to read his poetry. He shared his message that a person can do simple acts, such as being a volunteer, to bring peace and hope to the world.

## Regular Kid

Mattie worked hard to support MDA, promote his books, and volunteer at his church. Although his time was full, Mattie followed his own advice. He played whenever he could.

Mattie loved going to camp. Every summer that he was healthy enough, Mattie attended Maryland's MDA camp at Camp Maria. MDA camps are for kids affected by any of the neuromuscular diseases in MDA's program. The camps provide special activities, such as wheelchair football, so that all kids can get involved.

Mattie spoke with Jerry Lewis, the MDA national chairman, at the 37th MDA telethon. Mattie provided a lot of support to MDA.

Whenever he could, Mattie attended Camp María, a camp provided by MDA for children with neuromuscular diseases.

Mattie also had many hobbies. He created and built big structures with LEGO toys. He loved movies, particularly the *Lord of the Rings* trilogy and *Harry Potter* movies. Mattie also spent much time reading. His favorite authors included Harper Lee, Herman Melville, and Lois Lowry.

Mattie tried to appreciate each moment of his life. He was often in pain and aware that he likely would die early. Yet he did not let fear or anger rule his life. "I treasure that in spite of all the difficult things I have to cope with," Mattie wrote, "I am just an ordinary kid blessed with the extraordinary gift of daily life."[17]

# Chapter Five

# Mattie's Legacy

The years 2002 and 2003 were busy ones for Mattie. He was in and out of the hospital for various health issues. Still, he continued to travel across the country for his work. He read his poems, appeared on talk shows, and raised funds for MDA. MDA was so pleased with Mattie's work that he was asked to serve again as National Goodwill Ambassador in 2003 and 2004.

## Highlights

Mattie appreciated all of the exciting events during this time. One of his favorite memories was of the time that he and his mom went on vacation to Disneyland with singer Christopher Cross and his family. Another highlight of these years was that he met the actors from the *Harry Potter* movies on *The Oprah Winfrey Show*.

One of Mattie's activities from his MDA work was his annual appearance at the MDA's Ride for Life fund-raiser. Ride for Life is a

Harley-Davidson motorcycle event in which some 2,800 motorcycle enthusiasts participate. Mattie was impressed with the bikers' generous spirits.

Mattie grew excited about new projects as well. He met teenage best-selling singer Billy Gilman via satellite on the *Larry King Live* show in 2002. Following that show, the two worked together to make the album *Music Through Heartsongs*.

Mattie also started a project titled Just Peace. He began to write essays about what an everyday person can do to promote peace in the world. Mattie planned a project in which he would interview peacemakers around the world for their opinions. Through e-mails and talks, Mattie shared ideas about this project with Jimmy Carter.

A highlight in Mattie's life was his trip to Disneyland with his mother, Christopher Cross and his daughter, Madison (right), and Sandy Newcomb and Chris Dobbins (center).

# Physical Deterioration

By the end of 2003, however, Mattie had to slow down his work. His health took a major turn for the worse. He had to visit the hospital every other day for blood transfusions. By the spring of 2004, Mattie was admitted to the Children's National Medical Center in Washington, D.C.

Mattie's body began to completely fail him. He was in severe pain. In March 2004, Mattie went into cardiac arrest and then a coma. He woke from the coma but remained in the hospital. Mattie died in his mother's arms on June 22, 2004. His last poem, "Final Words," was spoken to his mother in May and June of that year:

> I am a man
> Of many thoughts
> And,
> I am a man
> Of many, many words.
> Have I done enough?
> Will it last?
> Amen.
> I love you.
> Yes.[18]

# Remembering Mattie

Mattie's funeral was held on June 28, 2004. People came from all walks of life to pay their respects to Mattie. The Saint Catherine Laboure Catholic Church in Wheaton, Maryland, was filled to its 1,350-person capacity by his family and friends.

The International Association of Firefighters (IAFF) are huge supporters of MDA. Mattie considered firefighters his family.

Dozens of Harley-Davidson riders and hundreds of firefighters attended. Mattie considered firefighters and Harley-Davidson riders his special friends. He had worked with many of them at MDA events.

Several famous people also came to honor Mattie. Jimmy Carter delivered the **eulogy**. He said that Mattie was the most extraordinary person he had ever met. Oprah Winfrey said that she believed Mattie was an angel on earth. She told people how Mattie wanted to be remembered. He had told her, "I want people to remember me someday and say, 'Oh, yes! Mattie! He was a poet, a peacemaker, and a **philosopher** who played.'"[19]

# Work Lives On

Mattie's work has continued since his death. Several scholarships, humanitarian awards, and MDA fundraisers, such as the annual Heartsongs Gala, have been named in Mattie's honor. Additionally, in 2007 the Mattie J.T. Stepanek Park at King Farm opened in Rockville, Maryland. When the park is fully completed, it will include ball fields, a playground, a concession stand, a dog park, plenty of green space and paths, and a statue of Mattie in his wheelchair with his service dog, Micah, beside him. Mattie will be sitting near a chess table with an empty bench on the opposite side.

The Mattie J.T. Stepanek King Farm Foundation also has been established to spread Mattie's message through

Jeni Stepanek sits with Kaylee Dobbins at the groundbreaking for the Mattie J.T. Stepanek Park in Rockville, Maryland. The park is dedicated to Mattie's message of peace.

ongoing peace programs and educational contests in schools and communities. The foundation works with schools and businesses to promote and celebrate peace.

# Words Live On

Mattie also had two books published after his death. His mother edited his writings. Jeni Stepanek copes with the loss of Mattie, who was both her son and best friend, by continuing his work.

Mattie's last book of poetry, *Reflections of a Peacemaker*, was published in 2005. The book became an instant *New York Times* best seller. In it, people including Maya Angelou, Jimmy Carter, and Larry King introduce each of the chapters of poetry. Oprah Winfrey wrote the foreword. A portion of the book's proceeds go to the MDA Mattie Fund, a fund established to help MDA research and programs.

Mattie did not have the time to interview peacemakers and complete his project, *Just Peace: A Message of Hope*. Instead, his mother pieced together his essays and correspondence with Jimmy Carter. Carter wrote the foreword to *Just Peace: A Message of Hope*.

In the book, Mattie writes about why there is violence in the world and what a single person can do to help stop it. *Just Peace: A Message of Hope* was released and became a best seller in 2006. In 2007, it was awarded the Gold Medal for "Outstanding Book of the Year" in the Peacemaker Category by the Independent Book Publishers. With this book, Mattie, even after his death, expresses his belief that people can rid the world

Through his books, Mattie continues to spread his message of hope and peace to the world even after his death.

of violence. "Peace is possible," Mattie wrote. "It can begin simply, over a game of chess and a cup of tea. I believe that peace becomes possible when we choose to make peace an attitude and habit. I believe that the reality of peace begins within each one of us, when we have our basic needs met and when we are satisfied with who we are as a person."[20]

# Notes

### Introduction: Introducing Mattie Stepanek

1. Jimmy Carter, "Eulogy for Mattie Stepanek," The Carter Center, June 28, 2004. www.cartercenter.org/news/documents/doc1791.html.
2. Quoted in Mattie J.T. Stepanek, *Reflections of a Peacemaker: A Portrait Through Heartsongs.* Kansas City, MO: Andrews McMeel, 2005, p. 3.

### Chapter One: Coping with Tragedy

3. Quoted in CBS News, "Disabled Child Keeps Going," September 2, 2003. www.cbsnews.com/stories/2003/09/01/earlyshow/series/heros/main571009.shtml.
4. MattieOnline, "Mattie's FAQs." www.mattieonline.com/faq.htm.
5. Stepanek, *Reflections of a Peacemaker*, p. 36.

### Chapter Two: Childhood Triumphs

6. Mattie J.T. Stepanek and Jimmy Carter, *Just Peace: A Message of Hope.* Kansas City, MO: AndrewsMcMeel, 2006, p. 18.
7. Mattie J.T. Stepanek, *Journey Through Heartsongs.* New York: Hyperion/VSP, 2002, p. 41.
8. Stepanek and Carter, *Just Peace: A Message of Hope*, p. 25.
9. Quoted in My Hero, "Poet Heroes." www.myhero. com/myhero/hero.asp?hero=mattieStepanek.

### Chapter Three: Three Wishes

10. Stepanek, *Journey Through Heartsongs*, p. 36.
11. Stepanek and Carter, *Just Peace: A Message of Hope*, p. xiv.
12. Stepanek and Carter, *Just Peace: A Message of Hope*, p. 28.
13. Mattie J.T. Stepanek, *Heartsongs.* New York: Hyperion/VSP, 2002, p. 25.

14. Quoted in *Religion & Ethics*, PBS, "Mattie and Jeni Stepanek," March 29, 2002. www.pbs.org/wnet/religionand ethics/week530/feature.html.

## Chapter Four: Spreading the Word
15. Quoted in Oprah.com, "Wisdom Beyond His Years." www.oprah.com/tows/pastshows/tows_past_20011019_b.jh tml;jsessionid=PJ.
16. Mattie J.T. Stepanek, *Hope Through Heartsongs*. New York: Hyperion, 2002, p. 49.
17. Stepanek and Carter, *Just Peace: A Message of Hope*, p. 22.

## Chapter Five: Mattie's Legacy
18. Stepanek, *Reflections of a Peacemaker*, p. 206.
19. Quoted in Stepanek, *Reflections of a Peacemaker*, p. xii.
20. Stepanek and Carter, *Just Peace: A Message of Hope*, p. 9.

# Glossary

**digestion:** The body's process of breaking down food.

**dysautonomic mitochondrial myopathy:** A form of neuromuscular disease that interrupts the body's automatic functions such as breathing, digestion, and heartbeat.

**eulogy:** A speech in honor of a deceased person.

**hapkido:** A martial art that stresses self-discipline and self-defense.

**humanitarian:** A person who promotes activities that will improve people's lives.

**muscular dystrophy:** A hereditary disease where the muscles gradually deteriorate.

**neuromuscular:** Having to do with the muscles and nerves.

**philosopher:** A person who offers views on questions about important life issues.

**spirituality:** Concern with religious values.

**trachea:** The tube in humans that connects the mouth and nose to the lungs.

**tracheostomy:** The construction of an opening through the neck into the trachea to allow a ventilator to be connected.

**transfusions:** Transfers of blood or other substances into a person's veins.

**ventilator:** A machine that breathes for a person who cannot do so on his or her own.

# For Further Exploration

## Books

Mattie J.T. Stepanek, *Celebrate Through Heartsongs*. New York: Hyperion, 2002. This is one of Mattie's five *Heartsongs* poetry books.

———, *Heartsongs*. New York: Hyperion/VSP, 2002. This is one of Mattie's five *Heartsongs* poetry books.

———, *Hope Through Heartsongs*. New York: Hyperion, 2002. This is one of Mattie's five *Heartsongs* poetry books.

———, *Journey Through Heartsongs*. New York: Hyperion/VSP, 2002. This is one of Mattie's five *Heartsongs* poetry books.

———, *Loving Through Heartsongs*. New York: Hyperion, 2003. This is one of Mattie's five *Heartsongs* poetry books.

———, *Reflections of a Peacemaker: A Portrait Through Heartsongs*. Kansas City, MO: Andrews McMeel, 2005. Mattie's last collection of published poetry.

Mattie J.T. Stepanek with Jimmy Carter, *Just Peace: A Message of Hope*. Kansas City, MO: Andrews McMeel, 2006. This title includes Mattie's essays about peace and correspondence with Carter.

## Web Sites

**Mattie Online** (www.mattieonline.com). The official Web site of Mattie Stepanek. It includes interviews with Mattie, the latest news about Mattie's books, and updates on related projects.

**Muscular Dystrophy Association** (www.mda.org). The official Web site of MDA. It includes information about how to volunteer and support MDA.

**My Hero** (www.myhero.com). This Web site is a not-for-profit educational project with a mission to inspire people of all ages. It has an Internet archive of hero stories of people, including Mattie, from around the world.

**We Are Family Foundation** (www.wearefamilyfoundation.org). This foundation creates and supports programs that inspire and educate people about mutual respect, understanding, and appreciation of cultural diversity. The Web site lists initiatives that involve young people, such as Mattie, who have inspired other young people.

# Index

# Picture Credits

Cover: Courtesy of the Muscular Dystrophy Association
Courtesy of the Muscular Dystrophy Association, 9, 30, 32
Photo by and courtesy of Sandy Newcomb, 38
Photo by and courtesy of Jennifer Smith Stepanek, 5, 8, 11, 12, 15, 17, 18, 19, 20, 21, 23, 25, 29, 33, 35, 37, 40

# About the Author

Leanne K. Currie-McGhee is the author of several books published by Gale. She resides in Norfolk, Virginia, with her husband, Keith, and daughter, Grace.